Through the EYES of a

NOBODY

...So I Thought

JERELENE
SHERONDA HILTONEN
JACKSON

CREATION
HOUSE
A STRANG COMPANY

THROUGH THE EYES OF A NOBODY...SO I THOUGHT by
Jerelene Sheronda Hiltonen Jackson
Published by Creation House
A Strang Company
600 Rinehart Road
Lake Mary, Florida 32746
www.strangbookgroup.com

Unless otherwise noted, all Scripture quotations are from
the King James Version of the Bible.

Scripture quotations marked NIV are from the Holy Bible,
New International Version of the Bible. Copyright ©
1973, 1978, 1984, International Bible Society. Used by
permission.

All dictionary definitions are taken from www.Dictionary.
com and www.Merriam-Webster.com.

Cover design by Bill Johnson.

Library of Congress Control Number: 2008929183
International Standard Book Number: 978-1-59979-390-0

First Edition

09 10 11 12 13 — 9 8 7 6 5 4 3 2 1
Printed in the United States of America

Me and my grandmother, Vivian Hiltonen

Have mercy on me, O God,
according to your unfailing love;
according to your great compassion
blot out my transgressions.
Wash away all my iniquity
and cleanse me from my sin.
For I know my transgressions,
and my sin is always before me.
Against you, you only, have I sinned
and done what is evil in your sight,
so that you are proved right when you speak
and justified when you judge.
Surely I was sinful at birth,
sinful from the time my mother conceived me.
Surely you desire truth in the inner parts;
you teach me wisdom in the inmost place.
Cleanse me with hyssop, and I will be clean;
wash me, and I will be whiter than snow.
Let me hear joy and gladness;
let the bones you have crushed rejoice.
Hide your face from my sins
and blot out all my iniquity.
Create in me a pure heart, O God,
and renew a steadfast spirit within me.
Do not cast me from your presence
or take your Holy Spirit from me.
Restore to me the joy of your salvation
and grant me a willing spirit, to sustain me.
Then I will teach transgressors your ways,

and sinners will turn back to you.
Save me from bloodguilt, O God,
the God who saves me,
and my tongue will sing of your righteousness.
O Lord, open my lips,
and my mouth will declare your praise.
You do not delight in sacrifice, or I would bring it;
you do not take pleasure in burnt offerings.
The sacrifices of God are a broken spirit;
a broken and contrite heart,
O God, you will not despise.
In your good pleasure make Zion prosper;
build up the walls of Jerusalem.
Then there will be righteous sacrifices,
whole burnt offerings to delight you;
then bulls will be offered on your altar.

—PSALM 51, NIV

I dedicate this book to the one true and living God with a Son named Jesus. All glory goes to God Himself for this book, *Through the Eyes of a Nobody...So I Thought*.

Thank you, Lord, for allowing me to be Your vessel; it is an honor. Lord, I also want to thank You for my late mother, Jerelene McDuffy-Hiltonen, and my father, Leonard Joseph Hiltonen, who instilled me with love, integrity, character, and how to be remorseful.

Contents

Foreword

THROUGH THE EYES *of a Nobody* will absolutely change the traditional paradigm of society's view of sexual and emotional abuse...Usually considered a taboo subject, *Through the Eyes of a Nobody* directly shines the light of truth on [the topic of] sexual perversion to expose the lies and strategies of the enemy. Jerelene Jackson has a sincere heart to see people set free from the condemnation, guilt, hurt, and bondage of a sexually abusive past.

The Word of God says we overcome by the blood of the Lamb and word of our testimony. Jerelene Jackson unashamedly divulges her traumatic history of incest and molestation in an ordained effort to help others overcome the pain and torment of a sexually abusive past. This book is a lifeline for those who are presently experiencing a dark, secret sexual life and have no hope of escaping.

Through the Eyes of a Nobody also serves as a spiritual warfare manual that underlines the crafty and subtle schemes of the enemy. Questions about homosexuality, transfer of spirits, rape, bestiality, etc. are all addressed from a spiritual perspective. I commend Jerelene Jackson for taking a stand to break the silence and speak loudly [the] truth and [for] giving the tools necessary to set many free!

—PASTOR RIVA TIMS
MAJESTIC LIFE CHURCH
6782 NORTH OLD BLOSSOM TRAIL
ORLANDO, FL 32810
WWW.MAJESTICLIFECHURCH.COM
407-296-8587

Acknowledgments

I WOULD LIKE TO extend a special thank you to my firstborn, Cedric, for helping all of his siblings; to my second son, Dedric, for helping with all the house chores; and to my third son, Sherod, for doing both. I also thank my younger children for being great balls of joy. I love you all the same. I would also like to thank my amazing husband, Sidney P. Jackson. Thanks to one of my sisters, Andreana. Thanks to my personal editor, Shontell Murphy, and to my hair stylist, Mrs. Christine Dunchie, who helped through difficult times. Thank you to Mr. James Yourree for giving me the right books to study; Mr. Long for providing the best Christian bookstore in Central Florida; Mr. Clement and the families that helped support our family while in transition, the Hill, the Nelson, and the Lewis families. Thank you to my mentors, my mom and dad, Mrs. Narva Woodard, Riva Tims, Michelle Decaul, Varian Brandon Boyles, and Pastor Denise Miller. Thank you, Pastors Victor and Barbara Goddard, for helping me in my deliverance. Jessica Leahy, you really believed in me. Mr. Allen Quain, thank you for praying with me and believing in me and allowing me to work with Mrs. Amanda Quain. She and I really connected. She felt my heart. Thank you, Amanda. Thank you, Ginny Maxwell, for praying for me, and thank you to Atalie Anderson and Jihan Ruano. Thank you to my eldest bro, Victor Lovell McDuffy. You always protected me when you could, believed in me, and loved me unconditionally. Thank you; you're the best. And Thomas Stacker, thank you for encouraging me, believing in me, and not giving up on me. You showed me I was valuable, and your family had that nice dinner for me when I got out of the hospital. Thank you Mrs. Mary, Jolonda, and Jesse. Thank you, to Mrs. Annie Parker and her son Corey (a.k.a. "Foo") for helping make this possible.

Introduction

YOU ARE ABOUT to be enlightened about the most swift and subtle demonic impartation, which is through sex. Also, you will learn how the devil assigns demonic spirits to you through people. I'm going to share with you how the devil, our enemy, tricks and lures us into demonic infestations without our knowledge or consent. The devil knows that if there is a violation against the principles of the Word of God—whether we know it or are ignorant of the violation in the spirit realm—we are still accountable for the choices that we make. The devil knows that he can't curse you, but he persuades you to curse yourself through sin.

The devil knows that sexual relations are one of the swiftest ways of demonic impartation. As a result of sex, two people become one with each other. It is a covenant through marriage according to Scripture, but today there are people who are not married legally but are having sexual relations as married couples do. They are becoming one with multiple partners, and before they are aware of it, they have taken on multiple personalities and are clueless as to how it has happened.

However, I will explain to you how the demonic impartation infested me without my knowledge or consent. As a result of incest, I was possessed by a demon. This began to occur in my life around the age of seven by an ancient demon, and it led to many other incidents, including an act of bestiality, a great deal of lying, manipulation, fighting, bitterness, rage, fear, feelings of shame, low self-esteem, theft, teenage pregnancy, and masturbation. These acts opened the door to astral projection, sales of illegal street drugs, suicide attempts, mental, physical, and emotional abuse. You will also learn how I became a silent murderer, slaughtering the innocent without going to jail.

Finally, I will share with you how the Lord delivered me from demonic manifestations, such as my reflection looking back at me in the mirror with a distorted image, and how my body levitated over my bed while the Spirit of the Lord supernaturally kicked a demon out of me, so that I could be swept clean for the Holy Spirit to dwell in me.

The things that I'm speaking about in this precious memoir, I actually experienced. My testimonies are not made up, but are true. I possess evidence of them—police reports and medical statements in hospital records. The above-mentioned occurrences, the doctors also found hard to believe because they had no knowledge of the demonic or supernatural realm. As you read these testimonies, which possess outstanding knowledgeable information, you will receive an extraordinary revelation of God's living Word, which will equip you for these last days by showing you how to recognize and eradicate the wiles of the devil. The Bible says that due to lack of knowledge, people perish. (See Hosea 4:6.)

I've paid a very high price. I've experienced a broken spirit, a broken and a contrite heart (Ps. 51). I will show you how the ways of the world beat me down and how God rebuilt and restored me for His glory in order to help liberate and set the captives free from the yoke of bondage through His anointing, His blood, the Holy Bible, and my testimony, which He had already predestined for my life before the foundation of the world, according to Romans 8:28–31, which reads:

> And we know that all things work together for good to them that love God, to them who are the called according to his purpose. For whom he did foreknow, he also did predestinate to be conformed to the image of his Son, that he might be the firstborn among many brethren. Moreover whom he did predestinate, them he also called: and whom he

called, them he also justified: and whom he justified, them he also glorified. What shall we then say to these things? If God be for us, who can be against us?

So that I do not cast my pearls before swine, I need you to examine your heart in order to appreciate how God had to rebuild me from being beat down and severely pained within my spirit and my physical body. Please understand that I a not calling you swine, but I am referring to religious folk and debaters that have mannerisms like the Pharisees and Sadducees, as well as unbelievers who may want to be critical about what I will share with you later on in the chapters that follow this introduction and my next book.

I would like the body of Christ to join me in the celebration of my deliverance. I thank the Lord for keeping me in the right state of mind, as well as for teaching me how to live a holy and sanctified lifestyle acceptable in the sight of the one and only true and living God, with a Son named Jesus Christ!

Chapter 1

Warning to Parents

WHILE I LIVED in Chicago, I had the experience of living on both the south and west sides of town. It was during that time, as a very young child around ages of five to seven, that I experienced incest. I cannot recall how it all started or with whom it started, but I can assure you that incest went on for some time in my very small world as if it were normal.

After a while, I became somewhat aware of what I was doing. I was aware that these acts were not supposed to be going on, simply because we had to hide when we were doing them. We were playing games such as "catch-a-girl-get-a-girl," which really meant you were to touch one another inappropriately in private places while fully dressed with whatever partner, girl or boy, caught or grabbed you. At that point, your partner would begin to grind on you. We used a lot of terms that meant to do these things with your clothes on.

We were basically a bunch of children performing a clothes-onorgy.

There were all kinds of games we would play as children in which we touched one another in inappropriate places. This would take place while the adults were in the living room visiting each other. The adults were not paying close attention to what we were doing. I also discovered that some of the other neighborhood children were playing the same games. We played what we called "house," which consisted of a boy and a girl, along with dolls portraying our children. This is what we thought grown-ups did as far as we could see with the eye. The things that we perceived that grown-ups did were things we saw on television, such as kissing and rubbing one another in private places. We also saw things in pornographic magazines that we found under the bed or under the bathroom cabinet. There were also times when we accidentally saw our parents in the act, but they didn't know we saw them. The places where these kinds of acts took place were in the bathroom, under the porch in the backyard, or most frequently, in the basement.

As I stated before, we were doing these immoral acts while our parents were sitting in the living room as we played in the next room or while they were at work, out partying, on dates, or shopping. They often left us in the care of someone they felt they could trust, such as our closest relatives or friends. During the time that we were in different homes, I do not believe that the adults were cognizant of this activity. I believe that the adults had confidence in our teenage cousins that supervised us while they talked or went out. If we were caught doing immoral acts while our cousins were supervising us or if we threatened to tell on one another, we were punished by our cousins with a whipping. They would also punish us by separating us or putting us into different corners of the house.

These acts began to happen repetitiously. Our older cousins did not tell the adults. We were basically introduced to sexual foreplay with our clothes on, rubbing against each other. I can assure you that we didn't realize that what we were doing was that terrible, but once we came into the knowledge that these acts were wrong, we tried not to do it again. At that point, blackmail came into play. If someone would not cooperate with the person who asked them to carry out this immoral act, they would threaten to tell an adult. At this point, you would either carry it out or run.

I would like for you to consider some of the harsh realities that our children are being faced with today. Parents, other family members, and friends, please don't underestimate your children or their friends, or your nieces and nephews, because this can occur right under your nose. You must not forget that they are little people with lots of knowledge. Please beware of what your children have been exposed to, whether it is television, music, or people with inappropriate behavior. According to the level of exposure that has infiltrated their ear and eye gates, they may try to repeat what they have seen and heard, just as we did. Please be careful. Children often know how to lie, manipulate, and keep secrets, so don't underestimate your young ones.

After being caught by a couple of older cousins while we were playing, eventually our clothes-on games became incest because there was an opportunity for the older children to manipulate the younger children into having sex with them. Instead of having clothes on, we had clothes off. This is when the game went to another level. I remember one of my cousins saying, "This wont hurt. Let's just do it a little bit." As a result of this "little bit," there was another element that came with this game, but it came from within. It was an embarrassing, overwhelmingly dirty feeling. I didn't want to play that game anymore, but the cousin I had sex with wasn't the only cousin doing this.

I had committed the sin called incest. I didn't know until God revealed it to me in the 1990s that an unclean spirit entered my body after having sex with my cousin. The Lord revealed where the unclean spirit had come from after many years.

Though it was years before I understood what

happened to me spiritually, I understood right after my cousin and I had sex that I could not tell about what happened, even though no one told me not to! I couldn't tell my daddy, because I was afraid somebody would have gotten hurt very badly. My dad didn't play any games. My dad was unaware of any of these things that were going on. Not to mention, my mother would have probably broken my neck, just as many other parents would have.

I will say that some parents are in denial when their children come to tell them about this behavior. When it is a relative, like the dad (or stepdad), the mom (or stepmom), sister, brother, uncle, aunt, cousin, friend of the family, foster parents, or something beyond the range of ordinary knowledge or understanding most people are afraid to tell. Also, some victims don't tell because the person violating them might have threatened their life. I've even heard of sexual offenders going to the extreme of terrifying the victim. For example, they may kill a small animal in front of the victim to scare them, telling them that this is what will happen to them if they tell. I also personally know a young lady who was repeatedly raped by her uncle. After he was done raping her, he hung her over a balcony, holding her only by her ears and head as a scare tactic. He told her that he would drop her if she ever told on him. She did tell when she became much older, but due to the fact that she was slightly mentally challenged, no one believed her.

When the spirit of fear has infiltrated the minds of these victims, fear begins to counsel their thoughts and emotions. This is the way to keep someone in bondage mentally, spiritually, physically, and emotionally. The victims are afraid to tell someone very close to them for fear they will be called a liar or that they will be overlooked and mistreated. The victim may even fear that they will have to look their attacker in the face at some point because of the events that have taken place.

Sometimes parents or guardians may know exactly what's going on and refuse to help the abused child because of fear, the stresses of life, or because it is a reflection of what they once were. There are also parents who have a nonchalant attitude about protecting their children. They may think, "I've been there and have gotten through it, and they can too!" There are other people who just plainly know their son or daughter is being abused, but they turn their backs for fear of losing their partner, who is hurting their children. I would also like to expose the dirty truth about some parents selling their children as prostitutes—little boys and girls being sold in order to feed their parents' habit of drugs or to help the family make money. As the Word of God says in 2 Timothy 3:2, 6–7, these parents become "lovers of their own selves.... [who are taken by] they which creep into houses and lead captive silly women laden with sins, led away with divers lusts, Ever learning, and never able to come to the knowledge of the truth." Even though this verse talks about women, I would also like to include men; they can also be lead away captive.

What people don't understand is that there is an innocent kind of freedom that God has given us naturally as children. Sometimes parents and guardians aren't free on the inside any longer like they were as a child due to broken relationships, abuse, envy, anger, strife, resentment, unforgiveness, bitterness, hatred, jealousy, rejection, and most of all disbelief in the Lord, Jesus Christ. Some people allow these spirits to counsel (advise) their hearts and minds, which affects their emotions. As a result, our little boys and girls have suffered and still suffer tremendously due to false emotions. Parents allow their children to be destroyed from within. I use the term *false emotions* because our emotions lie to us and have the power to make us harbor false ("not true, misleading, not real; artificial in a false manner") feelings and emotions.

We also have to understand that God has given us the privilege of parenthood. We have an obligation as well as a responsibility to obey God's principles when it comes to raising a child in the way he or she should go.

(See Proverbs 22:6.) In Mark 9:42–44 Jesus Himself says, "And whosoever shall offend one of these little ones that believe in me, it is better for him that a millstone were hanged about his neck, and he were cast into the sea. And if thy hand offend thee, cut it off: it is better for thee to enter into life maimed, than having two hands to go into hell, into the fire that never shall be quenched: Where their worm dieth not, and the fire is not quenched."

You may think it strange, but children actually know who they are at an early age. They walk in pure confidence, boldly proclaiming with their lifestyle the freedom that God has given them. As small as they are, they're fearless of most things. We read about this in Psalm 139:14, which says, "I will praise thee; for I am fearfully and wonderfully made: marvellous are thy works; and that my soul knoweth right well." Children naturally walk this scripture out with boldness.

Chapter 2

What the Bible Says About Incest

I F INCEST IS something that you or someone you know have experienced or are currently experiencing, it's wrong. It is an abomination to God, but if you are being forced into this kind of immorality, do not blame yourself. Your spirit is being filled with the filth of unclean spirits, causing you to defile and dislike yourself and others. Get confidential, sound, biblical help immediately. There has been an attack launched out against you because you are a precious gift. You were born and destined for greatness.

Let's briefly take a look at what the Bible says about incest, starting with Leviticus 18:5–30. It states how God our Father wants us to follow His decrees, and He then says no one is to approach anyone who is near of kin to him. In other words, do not have relations with your mother, father, sister, brother, cousin, uncle, niece, nephew, daughter, or son. Also, do not have sexual relations with your brother's wife or sister's husband. They are close relatives, and that is wickedness in the Lord's sight. The Word of the living God says not even to have sexual relations with your neighbor's wife and defile yourself with her. Do not take your wife's sister as a rival and have sexual relations with her while your wife is living.

There are more scriptures below that give proof that God is displeased with incest. As you read the story of Amnon and Tamar, found in 2 Samuel 13–14, you will see how the ruler spirit (Eph. 6:12) and the power of the darkness of this world can distort your thinking and cause you to give way to seducing spirits and false doctrines of devils. Amnon violently raped his half-sister against her will, causing her to live a desolate life. He gave in to the spirit of lust because he was dwelling on the fact that his half-sister was beautiful.

The Bible says that Amnon loved Tamar (2 Sam. 13:1), but Amnon allowed the spirit of lust to counsel his mind, which caused him to be vexed. Amnon knew that his half-sister was of a royal priesthood and that he could not treat her as a concubine, but his imagination was vivid with the vision of him and his sister in a sexual manner. His lust caused him to believe that he was sick with love, when it was simply lust for his half-sister. He could not distinguish love from lust. According to 1 Corinthians 13:4–8, "Love is patient, love is kind. It does not envy, it does not boast, it is not proud. It is not rude, it is not self-seeking, it is not easily angered, it keeps no record of wrongs. Love does not delight in evil but rejoices with the truth. It always protects, always trusts, always hopes, always perseveres. Love never fails" (NIV). Lust is "an uncontrolled or illicit sexual desire, appetite; lecherousness, a passionate, over-mastering desire or craving." Also, lust is the gratification of fleshly, soulish desires, appetites, and cravings. Lust is a cancer of the soul. Psalm 106:15 says lust produces leanness of the soul, so that after it has completed its assignment, it brings sin and then death. (See James 1:15.)

Amnon talked to his good friend Jonadab, who was also his cousin, and spoke into the atmosphere his desire to sleep with his half-sister, and it came to pass because the Bible says that you have what you say (Mark 11:23). Jonadab encouraged Amnon and told him a way to commit the act, which was ungodly counsel. We must be careful from whom we seek counsel. Amnon was in counsel with evil and took heed to it. He came into agreement with the voice of a stranger, which God says His sheep should not follow. Ignorant of his son's plan, King David summoned his daughter Tamar to attend to Amnon, who was pretending to be sick, but Tamar was unaware that she was being set up for what I call one of the cruelest acts that someone could plot.

Tamar was a virgin, but Amnon had already contemplated how to have his way with her, opening the door to a seducing spirit of lust to come in. James 1:14–15 says, "But every man is tempted, when he is drawn away of his own lust, and enticed. Then when lust hath conceived, it bringeth forth sin: and sin, when it is finished, bringeth forth death." As you can see, Amnon was not a virgin as his half-sister was, because he went into deep thoughts about a way to manipulate her. I believe that he had been involved in other sexual relationships because his appetite for lust had to be fed.

Tamar pleaded with him not to do this wicked thing to her. She told him to ask for her in marriage, but he refused to listen to her and raped her anyway. After he raped Tamar, he threw her out of the house. In the same chapter where we read that Amnon said he loved his half-sister, the Bible records that "Amnon hated her exceedingly; so that the hatred wherewith he hated her was greater than the love wherewith he had loved her. And Amnon said unto her, Arise, be gone" (2 Sam. 13:15).

Second Corinthians 10:5 states, "Casting down imaginations, and every high thing that exalteth itself against the knowledge of God, and bringing into captivity every thought to the obedience of Christ." You must be aware that we war against principalities, rulers of darkness, spiritual wickedness in high places, and unseen things. So let's keep in mind that according to 2 Corinthians 10:3–4, "Though we walk in the flesh, we do not war after the flesh: (For the weapons of our warfare are not carnal, but mighty through God to the pulling down of strong holds)." Amnon was being influenced by the ruler spirit and the power of darkness that is spoken of in Ephesians 6:12.

As a result of the rape and incest that Amnon committed, there was a devastating outcome. Because Amnon entertained the spirit of lust, his family suffered the consequences. Amnon was murdered by his own half-brother Absalom. After the rape of his sister Tamar, Absalom was filled with the spirit of anger and bitterness. He harbored these feelings for two years. These feelings caused him to murder his own half-brother. He was also angry with his father, King David, and attempted to dethrone him. King David mourned for his children because Amnon allowed the ruler spirit, the ungodly counsel of his cousin Jonadab, and the power of darkness to overtake him. After the death of Absalom, Tamar lived a desolate life.

I really want you to understand how the devil uses and influences people to carry out wicked schemes and plans. According to Ephesians 6:12, "We wrestle not against *flesh and blood*, but against *principalities*, *against powers*, against *the rulers of the darkness of*

this world, against *spiritual wickedness* in *high places*"*
(emphasis added). In other words, its not people we're
in a war with; it's the devil and his cohorts.

The devil camouflages himself through people. Allow
me to share something very important with you: the
devil's agents, who are demon spirits, need a body to
carry out some of their work. Oftentimes, the spirits
use the body of someone we are close to, trust, or who
may be familiar with us. For example, the devil tries
to blind us by using another human being to abuse
us. Naturally, we look at the person who has hurt us,
totally unaware of the assignment of the spirit that had
the power to influence the person who has abused us.
We can refer to this spirit as a ruler of darkness. This
kind of attack would have to come from another world
because another human being wouldn't be capable of
committing such a horrific act without the influence of
the ruler spirit. There was a door open for the spirit to
come in to inhabit the abuser. I'm trying to reveal to you
how the devil actually possesses people. Once the devil
assigns demonic spirits according to your weakness,

---

* **Definitions**: *People*: flesh and blood. *Principalities*: an order of, position
of, authority of, a state ruled by a prince who is also an angel. *Against*: in
opposition to, contrary to. *Powers*: the ability or capacity to act or perform
effectively; powers of concentration; the ability or official capacity to exer-
cise control; a persons, group or nation having great influence or control
over others. *The rulers of the darkness of this world*: a person who governs,
rule by right of authority, influence over; the motives governing a decision.
Spiritual wickedness: wicked or evil; forces of the darkness.

he then influences or possesses other people to abuse you. As a result, you are left to ponder what has just happened. Even though it appears to be the person that has abused you, it's the devil carrying out his wicked schemes through people that he has assigned to you.

He has assigned these demonic spirits to you to try to keep you off focus, and his ultimate goal is to keep you from fulfilling your complete destiny. If the devil can get you to wallow in unforgiveness, bitterness, resentment, or hatred, he has legal right to influence your atmosphere to a certain degree. The devil comes to deceive you, destroy you, steal from you, and try to influence you to commit suicide spiritually and physically. The devil doesn't want you to know the truth. The truth is that the devil, whose name is Satan, has set you up to hate others and to have an unforgiving heart so that God Almighty can't apply His biblical principles to our lives. If you refuse to forgive, God Almighty can't forgive you.

I do decree and declare a full deliverance from the Lord Jesus over your life. I have already prayed for you, that according to Psalm 138:8 the Lord would perfect that which concerns you. So I implore you to fall down on your knees and repent in the name of Jesus if you have harbored unforgiveness in your heart toward the person or people who have hurt you. This can be a very emotional process, so therefore if you feel the urge to weep, please do so. Weeping is a sign of a broken spirit and a broken and contrite heart. (See Psalm 51:17.) Make this confession out loud with me and mean it in your heart so that you may be released from the bewitching powers that you have given others over you. Even if you don't mean it at first, continue to speak it into existence. Now repeat after me:

> *I forgive all those who hurt me, and I place all past hurt and unforgiveness on the altar and under the feet of Jesus. I seal my life with the precious blood of Jesus Christ. In Jesus' name I pray, amen!*

What you have to understand is that a true confession through the mouth is good for the soul. Now allow the Lord to reveal Himself to you and show you how much you mean to Him. Allow the Lord to reveal who you really are. The enemy doesn't want you to know who you are because once you come into full knowledge of who you are you can fulfill your destiny in life. At that point, the devil cannot keep you spiritually, emotionally, or physically bound through the suppression of your identity.

The devil knows your potential as well as some of the plans God has for your life, but no one knows the plan God has for your life like God knows it. Jeremiah 29:11 states, "For I know the thoughts that I think toward you, saith the LORD, thoughts of peace, and not of evil, to give you an expected end." God wants you to be free.

> If the Son therefore shall make you free, ye
> shall be free indeed.
>
> —JOHN 8:36

He sent His one and only Son, Jesus, to set the captives free. The enemy knows you're going to bruise his head and snatch God's people right out of his belly. That's why he has to camouflage his presence in your life. The devil's plan is to condition you ("to make [you] accustomed to") to believe that you are a nothing or nobody as a result of what you have gone through in your life. But I've come to tell you, you are the head and not the tail. You are more than a conqueror according to Romans 8:37. So please hold your head up high, never looking down low but pressing toward that mark that Paul spoke about in Philippians 3:14 and never looking back.

In Luke 9:62 Jesus Himself states that "no man, having put his hand to the plough, and looking back, is fit for the kingdom of God." God Almighty brought you out to help deliver His people due to the fact that you can overcome by the word of your testimony and the blood of the Lamb, who is Jesus Himself. (See Revelation 12:11.) Don't worry about how shameful, dirty, nasty, or lowdown you currently feel or have felt. Again as I stated earlier, do not look back. Don't worry about the past tricks of the enemy, but be thankful you're able to see the goodness of the Lord in the land of living (Ps. 27:13) and to see Him

21

setting you free. If the devil afflicted you to this degree, it is a sign that you are born for greatness.

You were born to bruise ("to injure the surface of, causing spoilage, denting, etc.") the devil's head and cause spoilage to his plans. God uses His Word and people to set the captives free. Allow me to encourage you. The Bible says in Psalm 34:19, "Many are the afflictions of the righteous: but the LORD delivereth him out of them all." So, you have something to bless the Lord about at all times, and His praise shall continually be in your mouth. The fight is fixed. The battle is not yours; it's the Lord's, and it's already won.

I would like to lead you in a prayer of repentance:

Lord, I repent in the name of Jesus for my sins and iniquities from my deepest, innermost being. I forgive all those who have mistreated, hurt, or abused me in any way. I release all anger, hostility, bitterness, resentment, hate, and unforgiveness right now. I take authority over these spirits and their cohorts, and I command them to lose me in the name of Jesus. I bind every vain imagination, every ruler spirit and power of darkness, and any unseen forces that will attempt to influence me in my decision to forgive in Jesus' name. I bind every spirit of backlash and retaliation that would try to rise up against me. I apply the blood of Jesus over myself in Jesus' name. Amen.

Chapter 3

Be Watchful

As I was explaining before, parents, please don't allow your children to spend the night out with friends while they're so young. I understand that you need time away from them, but please be mindful of who they are associated with. Please get to know the parents of your children's friends and visit the home. After you've done all these things, please pray for their protection before you allow them to spend the night out. Please make sure you know who is keeping an eye on your children while they are in someone else's care.

It is disgusting and hurtful to even think or talk about incest, molestation, or rape, just to name a few possible outcomes; but it's happening, and children are dying spiritually and physically as a result of it. I'm not saying you shouldn't go out to enjoy life. I'm just saying, be mindful of who you're dealing with when it comes to family, friends, or associates. This limits the opportunities that they have to indulge in indecent sexual activity.

Another point that I would like to make is that you have to be careful about allowing your children's friends to spend the night at your house as well. A girl who was my childhood friend spent the night at our house when I was in fifth grade. We went to sleep, but I awakened in the middle of the night thinking that I was dreaming because this girl was on top of me. I aggressively pushed her off of me. I was ready to fight. I was already very angry on the inside as a result of the things that had come against me in the past. I told her to not touch me ever again. I attempted to tell her mom and mine; but she begged me not to, so I didn't. I kept that incident to myself, but we could never have the friendship that we had ever again because at that point I knew she wasn't trustworthy. This girl never knew what I had already come out of.

Allow me to remind you that this happened in the comfort of my own home. We were at an age where we were completely knowledgeable of what she had attempted to do. I knew what sex was, but a girl on top of you—I just knew this was wrong. Two people of the same sex engaging in this kind of thing, that is really against God's plan for mankind. It wasn't right at all. I felt disgusted. I felt a different kind of disgusting, one that made me say, "Ugh!"

I remember one day my sister was taking care of me. We were at her friend's house across the street from where we lived at the time. I ran home to get something. When I arrived at our house, one of my oldest brother's associates came to our house looking for him, and my oldest brother wasn't home. I was alone when my brother's friend came by our house. Just that fast, he was able to take advantage of me while no one was around. He was about sixteen or seventeen, and I was about seven years old. He began chasing me, as if he were playing with me around the yard. Then he picked me up, and I began to hold on to him in a straddle-like position with my legs wrapped around his waist. He began to push my waist down, and he began to get aroused. We were fully dressed.

At the time I wasn't really scared about what he was doing because I was familiar with this type of activity from previous experiences with incest in the past. However, I was very uncomfortable with him trying to take me around the corner while carrying me. Things began to happen so fast, but a neighbor who lived on the corner came outside, and I said, "Hello, Mrs. So and So." She said, "Hi. Where are you going?" Then he put me down and walked away quickly. I never saw him again. I ran back to my sister's friend's house, where she was practicing for a high school talent show. We lived in a prestigious neighborhood where the neighbors knew and respected one another. As a matter of fact, a police officer lived directly across the street from our house. Doctors and lawyers lived in our neighborhood as well. Was I scared? Yes! Did I tell? No!

As I was writing this book, I stumbled across other family incidents. I found out about how one of the same relatives who persuaded me into incest also persuaded another relative into the same trap, but that time they were the same sex: male and male. I became aware of this some years later after our family relocated to Florida. In this particular situation, it wasn't only incest; this was an act of sodomy, which is an abomination in the eyes of God. God destroyed a whole city called Sodom and Gomorrah for sexually immoral acts such as this. (See Genesis 18–19.) It doesn't matter what you call it; though some prefer the friendlier term, homosexuality is sodomy. It is an act of sexual immorality.

My relative was struggling with the spirit of sexual perversion. Let me put it into real-life terms for you: this spirit is a demon being imparted through sex. This demon comes full-force to try to abort your destiny at an early age. Satan assigns demons to your life to corrupt, defile, and to deceive you into aborting the appointed destiny that God put into you before the foundations of this world. He plays tricks with your mind by attempting to make you believe you are a woman when you are born a man, or you are a man when you where born a woman.

Any time you are violated with a sexual assault, you feel the filth on the inside of your body. You feel it deep down. You know that something is there, but you're not sure what it is. I can assure you that it is a demon of filth, an unclean spirit causing you to feel dirty all the time. No matter how many baths you take, you never feel clean. This spirit causes your self-esteem to dwindle. You feel dirty and nasty inside and out. As a result of this type of sexual immorality, there is a deposit made into the person that has been violated.

This is also true with children. Sometimes we think our children are rebellious or uncooperative, but we must take time out to examine their behavior. It may not necessarily be obvious in the natural, but from a spiritual standpoint you will find out that there has been a demonic spirit assigned to them or there has been a spirit deposited into them. Over a period of time, it begins to manifest through strange behavior. Sometimes you will think that it's just the child misbehaving, but then it becomes out of control. You are not sure how to handle it. Some families opt for the easy way out by taking the child to the doctor so that the doctor can give them a diagnosis and recommend filling them with medication. This only suppresses the symptoms, leaving them depressed and oppressed. I understand that some people have not given their lives to Christ or may not have reached maturity in Christ so that they understand what their children are dealing with in the spiritual realm. Sometimes, the child is not able to explain what is going on inside of them, and they don't have the words to express what they are experiencing.

> Flee fornication. Every sin that a man doeth is without the body; but he that committeth fornication sinneth against his own body. What? know ye not that your body is the temple of the Holy Ghost which is in you, which ye have of God, and ye are not your own? For ye are bought with a price: therefore glorify God in your body, and in your spirit, which are God's.
>
> —1 CORINTHIANS 6:18

At times I take a few minutes to recapture the thoughts of my little cousin who was violated, how he used to be before he was abused. He was outgoing, very joyful, and displayed no signs of fear or identity unawareness. He was very confident that he could conquer the world. The little boy has grown up, and he has acted out what he experienced on a younger relative, a girl who contracted a sexually transmitted disease (STD) from him. He has struggled with thoughts of homosexuality.

I found all this out as I began to search and ask questions out of curiosity, because I wanted to know why certain events had taken place in my life as I was growing up. I needed to know what caused this to affect my life. Where did this impartation come from? How did I end up in a battle coming from within that I didn't know existed? I was actually in a war within myself. I understood that this battle wasn't mine; it was the Lord's. But I am also aware that the Word of God gives us instructions on how to prepare ourselves with the whole armor of God. This armor equips us to be able to withstand the wicked schemes of the devil.

As I discussed earlier, my female cousin was infected by an STD as a result of a male cousin violating her. I believe they were both under the age of ten when it happened. I was affected—I was infected with a demon of lust—long before these two cousins. Now, there was something this older cousin carried that was imparted into me and my younger cousin, the spirit of sexual perversion.

Spirits can be transferred from one person to another, just as HIV. Scientific studies provide that HIV is passed on from person to person through sexual intercourse. People can carry HIV (and transfer it to others) without experiencing the symptoms themselves yet. The same is true of people with demonic spirits. Some of them show the "symptoms" of the spirit inside of them, but other people can be infected with a spirit, even though they do not act like it.

The cousin who ended up with homosexual tendencies and I were both infested with something. This thing was imparted into us by our older cousin, which caused us both to go into disgusting, immoral sexual acts. For him it was homosexuality (sodomy), and for me it was an act of bestiality. These behaviors are not normal; these are unnatural and rare acts. This conduct is not permissible. It is sexual perversion.

This deposit from incest put me in a battle that came from within. I was not aware it existed. It left me confused, unstable, emotionally damaged, wounded, hurt, and distressed. All of my inner emotions were disfigured, because every time I looked at myself, whether it was in the mirror or in a photo I disliked myself. I felt different from anyone I'd ever met before. In other words, I felt like a scapegoat or a refugee fleeing from the abuse that I had encountered. I felt like I was in a prison from within. These ancient demon spirits tormented me for some nine years. These incidents caused me lose my true identity, nearly loose my mind, and to almost die a physical and emotional death. They also caused me to harbor anger and have very low self-esteem. I was never able to be or feel normal. Everywhere I went, I felt like I never fit in. I felt contaminated, vitiated, defiled, and polluted.

Chapter 4

Demonic Impartation Through Sex

'M ONLY SHARING this information for people to be
delivered and to show a pattern that demonstrates
how one of the biggest impartations of demons is
through sex. I also want to show how I became demon-
possessed by an ancient demon, which led me to
experience an act of bestiality that almost caused me to
lose my life. I'm talking about how when I was a nine-
year-old girl I was sexually assaulted by an animal. It
was all against the Holy Bible and can be explained by
the spiritual realm, which I will explain to you with a
diagram as an example later.

Christ bought us with His precious blood. Jesus
Christ our Lord paid the price in full so that we can
live an everlasting life. The Bible says our bodies are
of Christ Himself!

The Holy Bible says you are one with the person
you marry, and when you marry you consummate
the relationship. In this sense, *consummation* means

"to complete the union of a marriage by the first marital sexual intercourse." When I speak about being married, I'm speaking of a sexual relationship between a husband and wife, but nowadays we very often violate the spiritual principles God put in place by having a sexual relationship with someone who is not our spouse. When we become one with that person when we're not married, it's illegal according to the Word of God. The Word of God says in 1 Corinthians 6:15–16, "Shall I then take the members of Christ, and make them the members of an harlot? God forbid. What? know ye not that he which is joined to an harlot is one body? for two, saith he, shall be one flesh." Matthew 19:5 says, "'For this reason a man will leave his father and mother and be united to his wife, and the two will become one flesh [after marriage]'" (NIV).

Sex is spiritual. It may appear that you are just promiscuous, becoming more bold and stronger in your sex life. Maybe you believe the illusion that "Oh, I'm just experiencing failed relationships," but in actuality you are feeding the demon of lust. Its appetite is becoming bigger and bigger the more you feed it. The devil has convinced you to believe that you have gotten better at your so-called lovemaking, but all the while the demon of lust is becoming stronger and bolder. You are simply feeding this demon of lust and fulfilling its appetite with multiple sex partners. But the demon of lust is never satisfied.

The devil assigns someone to manipulate our body parts, causing us to desire what the other individual does to our body. When you allow your thoughts to be manipulated by the enemy in this way, you begin experimenting with all kinds of things. It is like you have just been set up by a spider waiting for its prey. You've been caught up in a web, and Satan is like a spider waiting for the right time to come and paralyze you. The devil uses the same strategy as the spider does, but he stings us and tries to paralyze us with hurts and disappointments in life. After a while you become beat down and broken as a result of the ways of the world. You have been caught up in the web of the sexual pleasures of this world.

But what most of us don't know is that any time you fornicate, you glorify the self, which is better known as self-glorification. Any time you give in to your will and not the will of the Father, you have just practiced self-glorification. Satan really knows how to break us down spiritually and emotionally by using the same individual that we've become so familiar and intimate with. He uses them against us to destroy our emotions and our spirit.

The person that you are involved with is also a victim in this case. Both of your bodies are being used as a paralyzing delay in your destiny. The devil uses this person to verbally, mentally, physically, spiritually, emotionally, and sexually abuse you. As a result of the familiarity of these types of abusive relationships, you begin to see yourself as a nothing and a nobody, unaware that Satan has assigned these counterfeit relationships in your life to steal your destiny. No matter how long or how many years you remain in a relationship that God has not ordained for your life, you will have been robbed of those months or years of God's perfect will for your life.

Because you are familiar with your present lifestyle, you may at times be afraid of change. When you are afraid of something, it is because of the spirit of fear. According to 1 Timothy 1:7, "God hath not given us the spirit of fear; but of power, and of love, and of a sound mind." Once we start to get fearful, we begin to rely on feelings, and feelings lie to us. Because we feel a certain way, we begin to think in the same pattern. We help bring forth the manifestation of that feeling by thinking that it is reality, but all it really is, is a vain imagination attempting to exalt itself above the knowledge of Christ. The Holy Bible says whatsoever a man thinks, it is so. (See Proverbs 23:7.) When you have wrong sexual thoughts, the devil is subtlety causing you to think this way. As a result, the devil causes you to go into sexual sin (fornication or adultery) because your body likes the pleasure that comes with that sin. That's why the Holy Bible says not to fornicate.

God knows that it is a trick to experience sex before

marriage. God also knows that you will enjoy sex. That's why He created sex for marriage. God is very adamant in expressing and explaining in the Holy Bible how you should wait for marriage and at that point experience sex. If we would keep these commandments, the devil wouldn't be able to use this act to lure us into sin against our own body, which is a way to keep us in bondage. I know that you are asking yourself, How is this possible? He is going to use the very act of sexual sin that you've committed to give you the strong desire to indulge in sex. When you are involved in this type of lifestyle, it becomes easy to engage in sexual sin with just about anyone. We can refer to this as manipulation to your body, a form of control. We know this as witchcraft in the Holy Bible.

As a result of the disappointing emotions that you have experienced, when you lie down with someone, that's when a wall has been created and your feelings become numb; then you are not able to recognize true love. What's really happening is that you have allowed different demonic spirits to be imparted into your spirit, soul, and body through sex. Now let's be mindful that whomever you are sexually involved with, they are now taking on some of the characteristics of the people that you are having or have had sexual relations with, including yourself. After taking on these characteristics, you are now subject to the manifestations of whatever spirits are residing on the inside of them.

Please understand that anytime you sleep with someone, you've just became one with that person—and you have become one with all those whom they may have slept with. Scientific research has proven with studies of HIV that if you have slept with an individual, you have slept with those same partners they have slept with.

Take for example Bob, who isn't a believer of Jesus Christ, who worships false gods, and has had five sexual partners that he has become one with. Those five people who have slept with Bob are Karen, Shawnta, Desiree, Mark, and Tabitha. Except for Tabitha, who was a virgin, they have all slept with someone other than Bob. Karen has slept with two different people. Shawnta has slept with five others. Mark has slept with ten people. Desiree has slept with seven people. Tabitha has slept with only one person, and that was Bob. Now they have all been contaminated with each other through Bob.

The sad thing is that Tabitha is a Christian and has slept with Bob, who claims to believe in God but doesn't believe in the God of Abraham, Isaac, and Jacob, who also has a Son named Jesus. Tabitha just thought she'd try what everyone else was trying, and she doesn't know how badly she's been affected. She's infested with all kinds of different spirits, and she doesn't even know it. One day she discovers that something is going on inside of her, but she is uncertain about what it really is. She has now begun to experience different emotions rising up on the inside of her, making her question who she is. There is a war raging on the inside of her, and she has not one clue as to what has happened to her.

She used to be a virgin who loved the Lord Jesus and was a very outgoing young lady. She was conservative, adventurous, fearless, confident, and has always operated in the spirit of excellence. Now she is withdrawn, bashful, timid, and lost in a storm of confusion. She doesn't understand how all of a sudden she changed and become someone she doesn't even know. Tabitha doesn't quite know how she became infected with this stranger living inside of her. (There's a stranger in her spiritual house, and it's taking her a while to figure out what's raging on the inside of her.) Tabitha didn't know that by having sex with someone who wasn't her husband, she become one with him. That someone was Bob—and all of his other partners.

Tabitha doesn't know that she has opened the doorway in her life for many demons to enter into her body. For example, we are all cognizant of the proven fact that you can contract a venereal disease (STD) such as herpes, gonorrhea, chlamydia, and HIV through sexual intercourse. We know that the above-mentioned sexual diseases are transferable through intercourse. When we look at this scenario from the spiritual standpoint, we see that it's not a disease such as HIV that is passed from spirit to spirit, but there are demon spirits being transferred into your spirit through sex, whether you have had one partner or multiple partners. Married or not, you are still open if you violate the spiritual principles in this area.

Here are a few examples in the form of diagrams that you may find helpful.

Bob: non-believer, Muslim   *Tabitha: Christian*

Bob

Bob has been involved sexually with five different partners. Bob is not married to any of the people he has slept with. Bob entered into a relationship with Tabitha, who is a Christian and a virgin. Bob had sex with Tabitha and transferred all of the spirits from his four previous sexual partners to her. Tabitha is not aware of the other people that Bob has slept with. Bob is also on the down-low (he is a bisexual male), so one of the four people he has slept with is a male.

Bob does not believe in the Lord Jesus Christ. Tabitha is under the impression that Bob is a Christian because he said that he believes in God. Tabitha is unaware of which god Bob claims to believe in. He's referring to a false deity by the name of Allah. That is why when you ask someone if they believe in God, you must specify the God of Abraham, Isaac, and Jacob, who sent His only begotten Son, Jesus Christ, to die for our sins.

Bob, Tabitha, Shawnta, Karen, Desiree, and Mark

*Karen has been sexually involved
with two partners.*

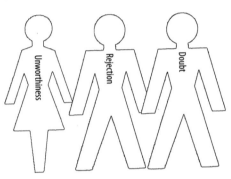

Karen has allowed the spirit of unworthiness to counsel her mind and spirit. She has never thought she deserved anything that was good. She was a victim of child abuse. She was constantly being beaten and told by her caregivers that she was nothing and would never amount to anything.

*Shawnta has been sexually involved with five others,
one of whom was a girl.*

Shawnta is a silent murderer. She has experienced incest at the tender age of thirteen when someone in her family raped her. She became pregnant as a result of this. She aborted the baby. She has also been exposed to pornography. As a result of all of these episodes, she is very hurt. Her spirit is broken and she doesn't trust anyone. She cannot understand how this could have happened to her.

After she was raped, she began to search for love in all of the wrong places. Her search began with people she thought cared for her. She has experienced a demonic impartation through sex. These spirits are counseling her mind and emotions. She desires to be free but does not know where to start. She is unaware that Jesus is the answer.

Desiree has been sexually involved with seven partners.

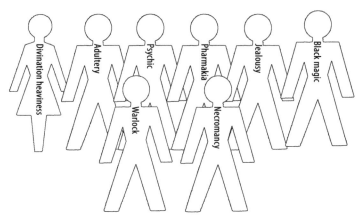

Desiree has been counseled by a spirit of heaviness because her family has been dealing in the satanic occult for many generations. There is a darkness that surrounds her everywhere she goes. She is bound within herself.

Mark has been sexually involved with ten partners.

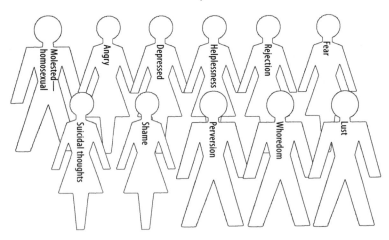

Mark was molested at a young age. His parents were consumed with life in general. They never spent any time with their children, and they always left them in the care of others. Mark was molested by another male, which transferred the spirit of homosexuality into Mark at the tender age of eight. Mark is troubled within himself, and he battles with a stronghold of lust.

42

He has an overtaking will to sleep with the same sex because of the molestation, but he is disgusted with men. He does not want to be attracted to men, and he is confused by these feelings because he wants to be married to a woman.

Tabitha has been sexually involved with one person, Bob.

Tabitha is a Christian who never experienced sexual intercourse until she met Bob. They dated for a while, and she was very fascinated at the fact that Bob is so handsome and has plenty of money. Bob seemed to be everything that Tabitha had prayed for in a man. He enticed her with words of affirmation and the fact that he said he believed in God. Even though Bob told her that he believes in God, he had never specified what god he believes in, which happens to be Allah.

Tabitha is nice, joyful, outgoing, very focused, and

is very in sync with her walk with the true and living God. Lately she was spending lots of time with Bob, and he coerced her into having sex with him. As a result, she has been infested with many negative emotions and spirits. She cannot understand where she has picked these spirits up from or why her perspective on life has changed. No one ever told her that sex is spiritual, and all of that person's spirits would be transferred into her if she became sexually involved. She doesn't even recognize that she has been infested with not only Bob's spirits but also those spirits from all of the people that Bob was sexually involved with as a result of her encounter with Bob. Tabitha also finds that strangely she's now attracted to women.

She begins to talk to herself, saying, "What is wrong with me? Why don't I have a desire to study the Bible or go to church anymore? I no longer understand the principles of God! I know what is morally and biblically correct, but why am I debating it? I know that I was taught sound doctrine, and I know that Jesus is alive and that He is the Way, the Truth, and the Life. I know no man can come unto the Father except through Jesus (John 14:6), so why am I second-guessing the Word of God?" Tabitha is not cognizant that it is the spirit of deception and the doctrine of devils, along with many other spirits, that have crept into her life. As a result of her disobedience, she no longer knows who she is.

These are some of the spirits that Tabitha has encountered as a result of sex with one individual, Bob.

These are some of the spirits that Tabitha has encountered as a result of sex with one individual, Bob:

The diagram above shows that everyone has something they're struggling with. These are just some of the struggles that are going on inside of the people on the diagram. Here you see that when you marry someone or just casually have sex with someone, you have just become one with all the different spirits that affect that person. These are only manifestations of different groups of demons that have just been imparted into you by having sexual intercourse, with or without a condom. You have just given the devil a stronghold in your life. Once again, how did you do that? You have done this by giving the enemy a doorway through sex, which is a very common way that spirits enter in. This is why the Bible says that you should not be unequally yoked with an unbeliever. (See 2 Corinthians 6:14.)

When you indulge in sexual activity with someone, you become one at that time. You become one this way because you violate the principles of the spiritual covenant that God has ordained for marriage only.

> "Everything is permissible for me"—but not everything is beneficial. "Everything is permissible for me"—but I will not be mastered by anything. "Food for the stomach and the stomach for food"—but God will destroy them both. The body is not meant for sexual immorality, but for the Lord, and the Lord for the body. By his power God raised

the Lord from the dead, and he will raise us also. Do you not know that your bodies are members of Christ himself? Shall I then take the members of Christ and unite them with a prostitute? Never! Do you not know that he who unites himself with a prostitute is one with her in body? For it is said, "The two will become one flesh." But he who unites himself with the Lord is one with him in spirit. Flee from sexual immorality. All other sins a man commits are outside his body, but he who sins sexually sins against his own body. Do you not know that your body is a temple of the Holy Spirit, who is in you, whom you have received from God? You are not your own; you were bought at [with] a price. Therefore honor God with your body.

—1 CORINTHIANS 6:12–20

I would like to lead you in a prayer for deliverance, healing, and freedom, which I wrote with the help of my friend Shontell Murphy.

Holy Spirit, guide me as I pray this prayer. I divorce every demon spirit that I supernaturally married by violating the spiritual realm through illicit sex. I renounce every demon that has entered my body through sex. I renounce every spirit that has been transferred to me through _____ (call out the names of every individual that you have been sexually involved with). I break every ungodly soul tie, and I command you to loose me in Jesus' name. I lay down self idolatry at the feet of Jesus. Self idolatry, you must go to Hades in Jesus' name. I apply the blood of Jesus from the crown of my head to the soles of my feet. I apply the blood of Jesus to every broken part of my spirit, soul, and body. Thank You, Lord, for keeping me in the right state of mind and healing my emotions from all hurt and disappointment that I have experienced as a result of the choices I have made concerning my body, which is the temple of the Holy Spirit. In Jesus' name, amen.

Chapter 5

Do Not Be Unequally Yoked

SEXUAL SIN OPENS you up to the enemy, giving him a direct stronghold in your life. One thing Satan understands is that he cannot curse the children of God. Let's refer to the story of Balak and Balaam in the Holy Bible. (See Numbers 23–25.) Examine how each time Balak wanted Balaam to curse Israel, but to the king's dismay Balaam blessed them and did not curse them. I will explain this further as you read on, but if you read the story in the Bible you'll find out that what God has blessed, no one can curse. According to Isaiah 54:17, "No weapon formed against thee shall prosper."

Please be mindful that the enemy's goal is to trick you into believing that sin is OK and that nothing is wrong with it. Beloved, I am here to tell you that anything contrary to the Holy Word of God is wrong. It's part of the enemy's job to deceive you, and what he does is cause you to commit sin in several ways. The devil knows that fornication, rape, molestation, incest, adultery, or any type of sexual perversion open the door for many of his deceitful tactics to infiltrate your life. These are some of the ways that you begin to curse yourself through defiling your temple, which is your body.

For example, when you are saved, your "house," your spirit, is considered swept clean. However, when you fall into sin after you're saved and you commit the same sexual acts with an unrepentant heart, you then receive more corruptible spirits—seven times stronger than the first.

While you're in the backslidden position, normally you have a heartfelt desire to change. In order to come back into right fellowship with God, you must first repent.

> If we confess our sins, he is faithful and just to forgive us our sins, and to cleanse us from all unrighteousness.
>
> —1 JOHN 1:9

However, some of us are so deep into sin and don't even realize it. I believe that's why God renews His mercies every day, so that we can have a chance at everlasting life. We should not become so familiar with our First Love that we think we can walk in and out of the covenant when we are ready. (See Revelation 2:4–5.) All He is asking for us to do is repent and live our lives like we did when we first became committed to Him.

Satan is aware that the flesh likes to feel good; that's why if you read the story of Balaam the sorcerer, you will see he had gotten greedy, and greed led him to manipulate and to trick Israel into having sex with the very Moabite women that God told Israel not mix with because they worshiped other gods. God knew that these women would turn the Israelites away from Him. Satan knew that he couldn't curse the children of Israel, but he could send his evil spirits on an assignment to trick God's people into sinning. Their sin gave him a stronghold so that he could get into their lives.

Remember, the flesh likes to feel good. When you please your flesh instead of pleasing God, you have just glorified yourself. Self-glorification is the same thing that caused Satan to be kicked out of heaven. He loved himself more than he loved God. The Bible declares that in the Last Days, men will be lovers of themselves, lovers of pleasure rather then lovers of God, having a form of godliness but denying its power. We are told to have nothing to do with them. (See 2 Timothy 3:2–4.)

As you can see, you should not engage in any type of sexual activity until marriage; it does not matter if you are a Christian or not. If you profess Christianity, you shouldn't marry an unbeliever. They must believe in the same God who has a Son named Jesus the Messiah as you do. Here are some examples of types of unbelievers: Muslims, Jehovah's Witnesses, Mormons, Scientologists, Masons, Hindus, Buddhists, and Satanists. They do not worship the Lord thy God, the God of Abraham, Isaac, and Jacob, who gave His only begotten Son so that we could have everlasting life.

Actually, when you engage in sexual sin, you became one with a spirit that is operating in that person against your God, Jesus. If you're not for Jesus, you're against Him. Please be careful whom you marry or have sex with, because they can cause you to worship false gods. They can cause you to debate and doubt God's Word. The seducing spirit inside of that person will be transferred into you to cause disbelief. You will begin to sense a breach in your spirit. When you try to seek God's face and you can't quite get into His presence or receive the breakthrough you desire, there's a force holding you back. Normally when you are in a relationship that is not ordained by God and you don't see the results that you expect from your prayers, it is because of the sinful relationship you have entered into. The seducing spirits that person has transferred to you keep you yielding your members to them instead of God.

Second Chronicles 7:14 states, "If my people, which are called by my name, shall humble themselves, and pray, and seek my face, and turn from their wicked ways; then will I hear from heaven, and will forgive their sin, and will heal their land." Also, James 5:16 states that "the effectual fervent prayers of a righteous man availeth much." Your prayers will be answered upon true repentance from the heart. You must purpose in your heart that you want the strength of the Lord to overtake you. The Lord will strengthen you, but you must let the sexual sin go and allow the precious blood of Jesus to wash and cleanse you from all unrighteousness.

As I stated before, the spirit of the Antichrist can cause you to stop worshiping the one true, living God. Here is some scriptural foundation on this impartation of demons that will turn you from our living God. First Timothy 4:1 reads, "Now the Spirit speaketh expressly, that in the latter times some shall depart from the faith, giving heed to seducing spirits, and doctrines of devils." Those demons will cause you to doubt and possibly worship their pagan gods with them. Here are other examples from Scripture of how demonic impartation through sex can turn you away from God.

> Do not intermarry with them. Do not give your daughters to their sons or take their daughters for your sons, for they will turn your sons away from following me to serve other gods, and the LORD's anger will burn against you and will quickly destroy you.
>
> —DEUTERONOMY 7:3–4, NIV

53

> He walked in the ways of the kings of Israel,
> as the house of Ahab had done, for he married
> a daughter of Ahab. He did evil in the eyes of
> the LORD.
>
> —2 CHRONICLES 21:6, NIV

Athaliah was Jezebel's daughter, and she brought her mother's evil ways into her marriage to Jehoram, the king of Judah. Look what it caused. There was prostitution, murder, and idol worship.

> In the time of Jehoram, Edom rebelled against
> Judah and set up its own king. So Jehoram
> went there with his officers and all his char-
> iots. The Edomites surrounded him and his
> chariot commanders, but he rose up and broke
> through by night. To this day Edom has been
> in rebellion against Judah. Libnah revolted at
> the same time, because Jehoram had forsaken
> the LORD, the God of his fathers. He had also
> built high places on the hills of Judah and had
> caused the people of Jerusalem to prostitute
> themselves and had led Judah astray.
>
> —2 CHRONICLES 21:8–11, NIV

> After all this, the LORD afflicted Jehoram with
> an incurable disease of the bowels.
>
> —2 CHRONICLES 21:18, NIV

Jehoram's marriage to Athaliah was Judah's downfall, not to mention the fact that he killed his six brothers. Athaliah, Jehoram's wife, worshiped idols. Jehoram allowed and encouraged the worship of idols. After Jehoram did all these evil deeds, the Lord afflicted him with an incurable disease of the bowels. In the second year, his bowels came out because of the disease, and he died a very painful death.

Do you see how he married a woman who worshiped other idols, and this caused him to worship other idols and encourage the people to worship other idols? And let's not forget that he murdered his own brothers.

> He had also built high places on the hills of Judah and had caused the people of Jerusalem to prostitute themselves and had led Judah astray.
>
> —2 CHRONICLES 21:11, NIV

If you read Nehemiah 13:1–3, you'll find out that it was written that no man of foreign decent (Ammonite or Moabite) should ever be admitted into the assembly of God in the temple. This was because they had hired Balaam to curse Israel, but our God turned the curse into a blessing. Balaam's idea was to turn the Israelites away from the Lord, so he advised the Midianites to send Moabite women into the camp to seduce the men of Israel. Because of this advice, God's people turned away from the Him, and they were struck with a plague. (See Numbers 31:16.)

> While Israel was staying in Shittim, the men began to indulge in sexual immorality with Moabite women, who invited them to the sacrifices to their gods. The people ate and bowed down before these gods. So Israel joined in worshiping the Baal of Peor. And the LORD 's anger burned against them. The LORD said to Moses, "Take all the leaders of these people, kill them and expose them in broad daylight before the LORD, so that the LORD's fierce anger may turn away from Israel."
>
> —NUMBERS 25:1, NIV

Now let's look at what the men of Israel had done. Numbers 25:1 states that the men first began to indulge in sexual immorality with the Moabite women. These women didn't believe in the Lord. There's proof that the men had sex with these unbelieving women *first,* then they were invited to worship other gods, which they did. Then the women invited them to the sacrifices to their gods, where the Israelite men bowed down and worshiped before the god of Baal Peor.

Because of their sin, a plague struck the Israelite camp. God ordered Moses to tell the Israel's judges to kill all the men who participated in the immorality and idolatry. (See Numbers 25:5.) Because of Jesus' sacrifice, we don't have to kill anyone; all we have to do is repent and confess our sin. Praise the Lord! First John 1:9 says, "If we confess our sins, he is faithful and just and will forgive us our sins and purify us from all unrighteousness" (NIV).

Now let's look at what our Lord told King Solomon about his foreign women.

> King Solomon, however, loved many foreign women besides Pharaoh's daughter—Moabites, Ammonites, Edomites, Sidonians and Hittites. They were from nations about which the LORD had told the Israelites, "You must not intermarry with them, because they will surely turn your hearts after their gods." Nevertheless, Solomon held fast to them in love. He had seven hundred wives of royal birth and three hundred concubines, and his wives led him astray. As Solomon grew old, his wives turned his heart after other gods, and his heart was not fully devoted to the LORD his God, as the heart of David his father had been. He followed Ashtoreth the goddess of the Sidonians, and Molech the detestable god of the Ammonites. So Solomon did evil in the eyes of the LORD; he did not follow the

LORD completely, as David his father had done. On a hill east of Jerusalem, Solomon built a high place for Chemosh the detestable god of Moab, and for Molech the detestable god of the Ammonites. He did the same for all his foreign wives, who burned incense and offered sacrifices to their gods. The LORD became angry with Solomon because his heart had turned away from the LORD, the God of Israel, who had appeared to him twice. Although he had forbidden Solomon to follow other gods, Solomon did not keep the LORD's command. So the LORD said to Solomon, "Since this is your attitude and you have not kept my covenant and my decrees, which I commanded you, I will most certainly tear the kingdom away from you and give it to one of your subordinates. Nevertheless, for the sake of David your father, I will not do it during your lifetime. I will tear it out of the hand of your son."

—1 KINGS 11:1–12

As we look at the wives of Solomon, the wisest man ever, we see that he fell into compromise with lustful desires and married the unbelievers, who in his older years caused him to worship other gods. According to 1 Kings 11:4–5, although he didn't worship the dead gods his wives introduced to him right away, he eventually worshiped other idol gods for the pleasures of his own flesh. Solomon had sex with his unbelieving wives, then he worshiped false gods. One led to the other. If it happened to Solomon, the wisest man ever, it could happen to us, so please live holy lives and do not mix yourselves up with unbelievers.

We can also look at Ezra 9:10–12 (NIV):

> "But now, O our God, what can we say after this? For we have disregarded the commands you gave through your servants the prophets when you said: 'The land you are entering to possess is a land polluted by the corruption of its peoples. By their detestable practices they have filled it with their impurity from one end to the other. Therefore, do not give your daughters in marriage to their sons or take their daughters for your sons. Do not seek a treaty of friendship with them at any time, that you may be strong and eat the good things of the land and leave it to your children as an everlasting inheritance.'"

God commanded Ezra and the people not to mix with those people. God said the land was polluted by the corruption of its people because of their detestable practices, and they had filled it with their impurity from one end to the other. They worshiped other gods, and God didn't want to mix His holy people with the ones who were filled with impurity.

So to all sons and daughters, menservants and handmaidens of the Lord, allow me to share God's Holy Word with you all.

> Do not be yoked together with unbelievers. For what do righteousness and wickedness have in common? Or what fellowship can light have with darkness? What harmony is there between Christ and Belial [this is another name for the devil]? What does a believer have in common with an unbeliever? What agreement is there between the temple of God and idols? For we are the temple of the living God. As God has said: "I will live with them and walk among them, and I will be their God, and they will be my people. Therefore come out from them and be separate, says the Lord. Touch no unclean thing, and I will receive you. I will be a Father to you, and you will be my sons and daughters, says the Lord Almighty."
> —2 CORINTHIANS 6:14–18, NIV

Since we have these promises, dear friends,
let us purify ourselves from everything that
contaminates body and spirit, perfecting holi-
ness out of reverence for God.
—2 CORINTHIANS 7:1, NIV

These scriptures that I am sharing with you are a
warning to us, to all believers who are born again, for
those who want to be set free from within, and to those
who want to come to know Christ Jesus. Please do not
intermarry with unbelievers as Solomon did, or it may
cause you to indulge in all types of sexual immorality
(like the Corinthian people did).

Paul also states:

So we make it our goal to please him, whether
we are at home in the body or away from it.
For we must all appear before the judgment
seat of Christ, that each one may receive what
is due him for the things done while in the
body, whether good or bad.
—2 CORINTHIANS 5:9–10

This is why it is very important to obey the Holy
Word of God. We should not go about fornicating and
sinning against God the Father with our own bodies
becoming contaminated and full of filth. The Word of
God tells us how to live holy lives before our Lord, who

bought us with a very high price. He performed the greatest act of all, which is love, by laying down His life so that we may live. He shed His precious blood for us so that we could live life eternally.

God doesn't want you to be confused, unaware of who you are and whose you are. I just want you to understand that you do not own yourself; but as I said before, you were bought with a price, the blood of Jesus Christ. God doesn't want you to open yourself up to false doctrines or a false sense of worship by becoming one with whatever demon spirit will be imparted into you through fornication, incest, rape, homosexuality, and bestiality, all of which are forms of sexual immorality. All of these sexually impure acts are considered strange.

John 4:23 states, "But the hour cometh, and now is, when the true worshippers shall worship the Father in spirit and in truth: for the Father seeketh such to worship him." God wants you to be able to come before Him and really worship Him in Spirit and in truth, but if you're committing fornication and receiving unclean impartations through filthy, contaminated demons, God cannot release Himself to you even though He desires to. You can't fully receive what He has for you when your temple is defiled with all types of foul demons.

Sin stinks in the nostrils of God. Just think if you've ever known anyone or if you yourself have ever contracted an STD. It has a foul odor. The smell is terrible. It stinks, and so does sin.

I really want you to see how many of us have been tricked and subdued by the enemy into believing that fornication, protected or unprotected, is OK. Everyone now is being encouraged to have protected sex, if they are going to have any. We're all basically told it's OK. But guess what? It's not OK. In fact, sex outside of marriage is sin. It's morally and spiritually wrong.

All over the world people are told that premarital or extramarital sex is OK and that all we have to do is strap up (put a condom on) and you'll be fine. Everywhere you go, the "experts"—the schools, the news health summits, and clinics—are promoting so-called safe sex. However, what the movies, news, health summits, schools, and clinics don't tell you is that sex is a spiritual thing, not just a physical thing; and, there are spiritual consequences for violating spiritual rules. As a matter of fact, they cannot tell you this because they are not in tune with the spiritual realm of God. The consequences for violation of spiritual rules include but are not limited to death; disease; infestation with STDs, including HIV; strong holds; and transferring of spirits.

I want you to understand that the secular world isn't teaching this, and some parts of the body of Christ aren't either. Why? Because a lot of people in the church are committing fornication, adultery, homosexuality, or some sort of sexual immorality. The church needs to be dealt with on this matter as well. Like Paul said in 1 Corinthians 5:13, "Expel the immoral man (brother or sister) out of the church" (author's paraphrase). I am not speaking of those who are going through true deliverance but of those who do not have a true desire from within for change.

> But now I have written unto you not to keep company, if any man that is called a brother be a fornicator, or covetous, or an idolator, or a railer, or a drunkard, or an extortioner; with such an one no not to eat. For what have I to do to judge them also that are without? do not ye judge them that are within? But them that are without God judgeth. Therefore put away from among yourselves that wicked person.
> —1 CORINTHIANS 5:11–13

Paul even says, "What business is it of mine to judge those outside the church? Are you not to judge those inside? God will judge those outside. 'Expel the wicked man from among you'" (1 Cor. 5:11–13, NIV). Paul is saying something similar to Psalm 1:1–2, which says:

> Blessed is the man that walketh not in the counsel of the ungodly, nor standeth in the

way of sinners, nor sitteth in the seat of the scornful. But his delight is in the law of the LORD; and in his law doth he meditate day and night.

Second Corinthians 5:17 states, "Therefore if any man be in Christ, he is a new creature: old things are passed away; behold, all things are become new." In Philippians 3:14 Paul says, "I press toward the mark for the prize of the high calling of God in Christ Jesus." We must be careful not to be entertained with what the ungodly are doing. We can be easily tempted or lured into what they are doing—even more by spending too much time with them, as well as participating in the things that they do. We should not be lending our ears to listen to them talk about indulging in the sinful acts of immorality that God has previously delivered us from in our past. We may become tempted to go back that way again if we are looking at their sinful acts. We must guard our eye gates and ear gates and not allow everything to enter into our spirit.

Please allow me to clarify that I am not saying that you can't go around your friends, coworkers, or family members that aren't saved. The Bible says that Jesus came to heal the sick. He came for the sinners, to set the captives free. However, when Jesus witnessed to them, He always witnessed a Word, healed them, and encouraged them. And He immediately dealt with the situation. He told them, "Sin no more," and at that point He left and went on to His next assignment. He didn't sit and allow them to corrupt His Spirit by hanging out with them while they participated in sin.

There were many things Jesus couldn't do because the people didn't want to receive Him, although they saw the great miracles that Jesus performed. He knew that either people want to change, or they don't. The Bible says to dust your feet off if the people you witness to don't receive the Word. (See Mark 6:11.) You can't force the Word on anyone, but you can live a holy lifestyle of worship before them. People are more open to receive you because of your holy lifestyle and kind ways, and God will use His Spirit to draw them through you. (See John 12:32.)

Me at nine years old

Chapter 6

My Encounter with the Demonic

I KEPT MANY SECRETS about the incest that took place in the basement and under the porches in Chicago. I knew how to lie and keep secrets at a very young age. But there was something that happened to me that I didn't cope with very well. It was not normal. I had never seen anything like this, nor had I ever experienced anything like this before. Please bear with me as I tell you this story from a nine-year-old's perspective, because that is how old I was when this horrible thing happened to me. It was cruel, disgusting, and immoral. It was something that almost cost me my life. This was an act of sexual perversion caused by the enemy. It left me bleeding and in a lot of pain physically, emotionally, and mentally.

My mom, brother, sister, our dog, Butch, and I were coming home from Lake Antoine in Iron Mountain, Michigan, over a hill called Millie. I remember we took a shortcut going through the woods running home.

My sister, brother, Butch, and I began to race to see who could get home the fastest. As we played through the woods, I was determined to win the race. I left my siblings and mother far behind, but Butch ended up following me.

As I ran, I was looking at the beautiful trees all around me. I was amazed at the beauty. I finally reached home, and I had won the race. While I was waiting for the others to catch up, I decided to check to see if we had left one of the doors open. The type of home we lived in was called a miner's house. We had about seven to ten bedrooms in that house. I remember having to go to the bathroom, but I couldn't get in the house because all of the doors were locked. I attempted to get in through the back porch, to no avail. Butch was still with me the whole time.

I found a coffee can to urinate in, and after I urinated in the can I noticed that there was this very dark presence that was in the air that I didn't understand. There are certain types of atmospheres in different places. For example, when you go to a nightclub, there is a lustful atmosphere. When you go to church, there is a peaceful atmosphere. When you go to the movies and see a horror movie, there is a fearful atmosphere. The atmosphere that I was in at that time was thick and dark. At the time I didn't know what this was, except that the feeling in the air was almost like there was someone on the porch with Butch and myself; but I couldn't see the other person. I felt the presence of something dark and scary.

Butch was backing up in the corner, squealing as though someone were beating him. Butch began making noises, breathing hard, and that's when he began to jump all over me like something had possessed him. It was unexplainable. It seemed to be something that Butch could see, but I couldn't. It seemed as if he were communicating with something.

The room was very dark, even though it was daylight outside, and I was being controlled by something that came from within me that agreed with the atmosphere. My inner being was being controlled by something, which I've come to know as a demon. I could not move my own body off the porch. There was something I couldn't see literally controlling me. I didn't know what was happening to me. Things were happening so fast. I was knelt down on the floor, unable to move.

While jumping all around while I was still on the floor unable to move, Butch began to assault me. "Ugh! Ugh! Ugh!" was all I could say or feel. Oh, how nasty and filthy I felt. "Help! Stop! No!" was all I could scream. Butch was breathing hard, slobbering out of his mouth, and sounding like someone was beating him. When he moved away from me a few minutes later, I collapsed flat on the floor weak, hurt, and disgusted. I wanted to grab Butch by the neck and try to choke him for what he had done to me, but I couldn't move due to excruciating pain.

I began to bleed. I was finally able to move after a few minutes, and quickly I found something to wipe my body off. I felt dirty and embarrassed. I was finally able to get up and get dressed, but I was still losing blood. I left the back porch and walked around to the front porch. Butch was by then lying down in the corner like nothing had ever happened.

Soon after this happened, I saw one of my sister's friends. He stopped and asked for a lighter or a match. I told him my sister wasn't home, so he left. Right after that, my mother, sister, and brother came home.

I was still in disbelief about what had just happened. I began to think, "Am I dreaming? Could this be?" The demonic force that was controlling me within began speaking to my mind like I was a zombie or something. This demonic force from within began to lead me to my parents' bathroom. I was trying to look as normal as possible. I went in the bathroom and began to run some bath water. As the tub filled, I remember putting some strawberry bubble bath in the bathtub, making a lot of bubbles in the water. I don't remember what I did with my clothing. I stepped into the bathtub in pain and bleeding. I thought if I put red bubbles in the water, no one would know or be able to see the blood.

Then there it was again; the dark presence had followed me from the porch. This demonic force made the atmosphere very dark and scary once again. I felt this controlling force coming from within. There was something similar happening to me all over again. I was being controlled by this demonic force, which forced me to wash myself off a certain way to wash away the evidence. After washing the blood away with the water, I don't recall how I was taken to the hospital, but I do remember my mom hysterically crying and holding me, asking me how this happened to me. (At the time, my dad was on a hunting trip.)

I remember being asked lots of questions by the doctors while I was at the hospital in the examination room. My mom had a look of worry on her face. At that time, I was being prepped for surgery. The surgeons began to repair the damage the dog had done to me.

Now of course, this incident was hush–hush. This was unheard of. Neither the doctors, the police, or my parents had ever heard of any such thing. The police had to ask me questions, but the answers they were looking for, I couldn't give them. This incident was a direct attack from the enemy. It was an unnatural thing. I know the way I explained what happened to me for the police sounded like a part of a horrible movie. There was an officer who kept asking me the same questions over, as if I had just made the story up. The same police who were supposed to protect me didn't believe me because of the nature of the crime. I was looked at as if I were covering something up, and I wasn't. I desperately wanted the police to believe me, and they didn't. I didn't know how far-fetched I sounded. I couldn't win for loosing. By telling the truth I sounded a bit confused, and my story sounded very fictional, although this really did happen to me. However, the police couldn't say that this was something that I had just made up, because there was surgery performed on me. I have police reports and medical records to prove that this horrible act took place.[1]

Later on in my life, I read a book that discussed ritualistic child abuse and found out that what happened to me happens quite often. I found out that in certain cults, especially the satanic cults, children and adults are often forced into this kind of ritual abuse. As a result of reading the book and talking to people while evangelizing, I found out that in some cults, children are being molested and introduced to sex at an early age. They are often first introduced to multiple sex partners, and as they get a little older they introduce them to sex with animals, which is bestiality. After bestiality they are introduced into sex with demons. Some of them become the bride of Satan himself.

Also, the Bible makes it clear that demons can inhabit animals and make them do things they would not normally do. I believe the way Butch acted on our porch before and while he assaulted me was the result of a demon influencing him, in the same way as the demons in the following scripture influenced the pigs.

They sailed to the region of the Gerasenes, which is across the lake from Galilee. When Jesus stepped ashore, he was met by a demon-possessed man from the town. For a long time this man had not worn clothes or lived in a house, but had lived in the tombs. When he saw Jesus, he cried out and fell at his feet, shouting at the top of his voice, "What do you want with me, Jesus, Son of the Most High God? I beg you, don't torture me!" For Jesus had commanded the evil spirit to come out of the man. Many times it had seized him, and though he was chained hand and foot and kept under guard, he had broken his chains and had been driven by the demon into solitary places. Jesus asked him, "What is your name?" "Legion," he replied, because many demons had gone into him. And they begged him repeatedly not to order them to go into the Abyss. A large herd of pigs was feeding there on the hillside. The demons begged Jesus to let them go into them, and he gave them permission. *When the demons came out of the man, they went into the pigs*, and the herd rushed down the steep bank into the lake and was drowned...When they came to Jesus, they found the man from whom the demons had gone out, sitting at Jesus' feet, dressed and in his right mind; and they were afraid.

—LUKE 8:26–33, 35, NIV, EMPHASIS ADDED

I know that you are probably asking yourself, What is she talking about? If I were you, I would say the same thing, but this is a harsh reality. I would like to explain what I have learned about the demonic realm.

When dealing with the demonic realm, there are different ranks of demons. Through situations like what I experienced with the dog, the devil uses carefully planned strategies to carry out his wicked schemes. Who would ever think that you could control people by using sex? I would never have thought of such a thing, but I do know someone who thrives off of our ignorance—the devil. He sets people up to have multiple sex partners because the more partners you have, the more powerful the demon of lust within you becomes.

The demon of lust is absolutely insatiable; he never gets satisfied, no matter how many times you have sex, watch porn, commit sodomy (homosexuality), commit adultery or indulge in bestialities. Lust doesn't have a gender; it's a spirit. As I said before, the spirit of lust is empowered through sexually immoral acts. That's why when you see someone who is out of control sexually—their hormones seem to be raging, as the world puts it, or you hear someone say that men need to sow their wild oats—that is a setup for a great fall spiritually.

We have to be mindful of these things because we expect to receive a wife or husband and give her or him the love that she or he needs and all of our undivided attention. But if you are not free of these demonic soul ties and the spirit of lust, the minute your spouse doesn't move a certain way in the bed, your mind will go to how you experienced that position with the other individual.

Chapter 7

How God Kicked a Demon Out of Me

I HAVE BEEN VERY blessed and privileged to have been delivered from the wicked schemes of the devil. Allow me to show you how God Almighty kicked a demon out of me.

There was a day when I was seventeen and selling drugs that I heard someone say, "You are hurting My people, so stop selling drugs." I looked around and said to my friends, "Did you hear that?" They responded, "Hear what?" I went in the house, and I heard the voice again saying, "You are hurting My people!" I looked around, but there was no one in sight. I said, "Man, what is that?" I put my fingers in my ears because I heard the same thing again, and I said to myself, "What is going on? I know I am not going crazy!"

I went outside and tried to ignore what had just happened, but I couldn't. I went back in the house and went in the bathroom and looked in the mirror. I remember asking myself, "Who am I?" while I was looking in the mirror. An older lady once told me if you look in the eyes of a person, you can see their soul. I began gazing into the mirror thinking, "Why do I feel like killing myself again? Why am I not good enough for my boyfriend? Why does he beat me up all of the time?" He was struggling with a crack cocaine addiction, and the nicer I was to him, the more harshly he dealt with me.

I began to have a flashback of when I was fifteen and pregnant with my first son. I wondered, why was I fifteen and about seven or eight months pregnant, and this man was beating me up? He would hit me with blows to each side of my stomach and hard-hitting blows to my face while I slept on the couch in the wee hours of the night. I couldn't think of anything other than that I must be a causing him a whole lot of sadness and misery because I got pregnant. "Maybe I'm holding him back," I thought, "or maybe I'm just not good enough for him."

As I continued to gaze into the mirror, I had another flashback of when I was pregnant the first time and my boyfriend was cheating on me. I had asked him about the situation when we were in the parking lot of a local grocery store. He began yelling at me, saying, "You better not ever ask me about anything like that again. That's my business!" I said to him while getting out of my mother's car, "You wait until I have my baby. I am going to find someone who is going to love me and treat me better than you!" Oh my goodness, he came on the passenger side of the car and grabbed me by my head while pulling my hair. He then slammed my head into a red brick wall so hard that I could literally see gray stars. Tears began to roll down my face, and all I could do was hold my head and my stomach. He had to help me into the car. I was overwhelmed with nausea and excruciating pain in my head for three days straight. I could only get out of bed to go to the bathroom.

When the flashbacks had ended, I began to think about why I was seventeen, pregnant again, and forgetting all the mean things my boyfriend had done to me. I was doing everything that I had learned to do in order to survive while living in the projects as far as street credibility. I was trying to be loyal and please my boyfriend; I was selling illegal street drugs for extra money so I could buy new clothes and shoes for him while he was in jail for beating me and trespassing. I made that boyfriend of mine a god unconsciously. I thought of him morning, noon, and night. Little did I know the one and true living God is a jealous God.

All of these things were going through my mind as I stared in the mirror with my eyelids stretched open with my fingertips. I was trying to see my soul through my eyes, as this lady told me I could do. I began asking, "God, if You are real, show me who you are and show me who I am. I don't understand my life. It seems that I am worthless. Please help me." As I started to walk out of the bathroom, I happened to look back, and there it was—my reflection was staring back at me. But that reflection of my face had a distorted look. I screamed, "Ahh! What was that?" I was running full-force out of the house, crying and saying, "Oh my! What just happened? Oh Lord, please help me."

Shortly after that, I got into a fight with one of my brothers, and I cut my brother on the hand. My mom called the police on me and told them that I was out of control, so of course I ended up in juvenile for a little while. While I was in juvenile, I met a number of people, including one girl who tried to recruit me into a satanic cult. The girl told me the devil is really nice-looking and that he would give me power to melt plastic, levitate, to get money, and so forth. She even told me there are people who pray to him like we pray to our God. I didn't know much about the devil, except for the fact that he is bad and that you don't want to deal with him.

This girl, on the other hand, had given the devil a name. She called him Satan, and I said, "Girl, you shouldn't be playing with the devil! How are you going to give the devil a name? You must be crazy. Get away from me!" I am telling you this to show you how clue-less I was about the devil. Then she replied, "I really like him. He is fine, and many of my friends have had sexual relations with him." I thought, "How is it possible that the devil can do that?" Then she described him, saying he wears a white robe and has long, blond hair and beautiful eyes. She said he looks like the picture that people have of Jesus. I stared with my mouth wide open in disbelief. I thought, "Why am I in this room with this girl who talks about participating in séances, barnyard fires, and rituals, as well as sticking her fingers with a safety pin and sucking the blood out of them?" I really didn't believe in the devil before that, but after that I was terrified because I knew the devil really was real and that people really worship him.

I was very frightened until I began reading the Bible, and after I began reading the Bible, I couldn't stop. I began desiring to know more about Jesus at the age of seventeen when I was pregnant. While in juvenile, I started saying prayers. I got out of juvenile and began to read the Bible day and night seeking for answers. I read about fasting in the Bible and began to apply the fast to my life. Before I knew it, I was feeling different. Things began to happen that I couldn't quite figure out.

I called my sister in Chicago and began to explain to her what I had been going through. Over the phone she introduced me to a pastor who operated in the gift of prophecy. When I spoke to this pastor, I was very amazed at the things he began to speak to me about.

I cried the whole time while on the phone, saying, "Oh my, does God really think about me?" After the pastor finished prophesying to me, I thought, "What an experience." I said, "My life will never be the same after speaking to this pastor." The pastor told me that God needed me to read some scriptures in the Book of Psalms that were prayers—Psalms 27, 35, 37, 91, and so forth. The pastor explained to me that what was going on inside of me was demonic activity and that God Almighty wanted to set me free from the yoke of bondage. The pastor asked if he could pray for me, and I said yes. This pastor was very informative. I don't ever recall him prophesying about material things but about only spiritual needs for my soul.

When I was finished speaking to him, I no longer thought I was crazy, and I actually began to have a sense of hope. I remember some of the things the pastor said to me. He said that the devil had launched out in the spiritual realm, and that he would come off of his throne to come kill me himself. While I was in tears, I asked the pastor, "Why does he want to kill me when I don't even know him?" The pastor replied to me, "God has called you to the End Times, and He will use you." I said, "He will?"

The pastor also told me to buy some 100 percent extra virgin olive oil so that he could pray over it. I went and bought the oil, and he prayed over the oil and asked me to anoint myself from the crown of my head to the soles of my feet, and I did. The pastor prayed over me and said that God really wanted to do something for me, and he said that I would not have to worry about trying to commit suicide anymore. My response was, "Wow! Are you sure?" He said, "Yes, and God is going to free you."

I struggled with being fifty pounds overweight, and the devil would really taunt me because I wasn't a size six or seven. The spirit of suicide rose up in me because of the pressures of life, trying to persuade me to commit suicide. I first attempted suicide by taking seventy-eight pills at the age of twelve, and I ended up at the Cook County Hospital in Chicago for several days. My mom, Jerelene McDuffy-Hiltonen, who loved me dearly, and my niece Danielle's father, Thomas Stackers, who was very encouraging to me, were at my side.

After the pastor prayed over the oil and I commanded the devil to loose me from the crown of my head to the soles of my feet, I started seeing some little flashing balls. This is the best way that I can explain them. The pastor gave me some instructions telling me, "You really need to read your Bible every day and seek God's face. Ask the Lord Jesus to come into your heart while you're on your knees in prayer." I said, "OK."

He prayed and spoke these things to me on a Monday. I got on my knees and repented, asking the Lord Jesus to come inside of my heart and free me from within. The next two days I read my Bible morning, noon, night, and in the wee hours of the morning. I was also still on my fast, at about the twenty-first day of the fast. I was not eating any food, watching any TV, talking on the phone, visiting friends, and definitely not listening to the radio. I was only drinking liquid.

Two days later, on Wednesday, I was babysitting a little girl who was about seven months old. I was also taking care of my first son, who was twenty-three months, and I had also just had my second child. I had just turned eighteen a few weeks prior. As I put all three of the children to bed, I began to read my Bible again before I went to bed. I fell asleep with the children in my white canopy bed with pink satin covers.

After a few hours of being asleep, I felt like I was picked up and moved to the middle of the bed. I opened my eyes and was not able to move. I was not asleep but awake. My body had a tingling sensation all over, from the crown of my head to the soles of my feet. Even my fingertips were numb. I didn't know what was going on, and I remember saying, "Lord Jesus, please help me. I don't understand what is happening to me." I was lying flat on my back, and I was in that position for approximately forty-five minutes, unable to move. All I could move were my eyeballs and my mouth to say, "Jesus, Jesus, Jesus! Oh my! What is happening?" I felt like there was something inside of my body tearing away from my inner being. What I felt was unexplainable. It was a separating of something coming from within, and this horrible thing jumped out of my belly as I levitated in the air. I didn't know it then, but God had kicked a demon out of me. When it left, my body fell back on the bed.

Once I was able to move, I crawled back to the top of the bed saying, "Lord what in the world was that?" I had a smile on my face and felt like a warm embrace was holding me. As I lay down, I then heard an audible voice saying, "This is how the Lord feels!" I jumped up out of the bed while rubbing my arms and shaking my hands saying, "Lord, what was that?" over and over again.

I looked in the mirror and saw that I was totally transformed. I said, "Who is that?" My hair had been stunted of growth and my skin was about three shades darker before this demon was kicked out of me. Once it was gone, my hair grew instantly and my skin tone became about three shades lighter. I had been about fifty pounds overweight, and the weight was gone instantly. (That is why I know for a fact that obesity is a spirit. Please forgive me if this is offensive to anyone. I'm not trying to offend anyone, but my goal is to see you set free, healed, and delivered.) I was totally transformed, and people were actually asking what happened to me. They all said, "You look so different, and you are glowing." Also, I no longer had the desire or the strength to fight like I used to.

Now you can see how the almighty one, true, living God delivered me by kicking out that demon that housed itself inside of my body. That demon had controlled me and tormented me for many years. Because I had recently accepted the Lord Jesus Christ into my heart as my personal Savior, the demon that was housed in me could no longer dwell inside of me.

I have also seen other people freed from demons that had infested and controlled them. One day my husband and I had a school meeting for one of our kids. He and I drove separately, and I arrived there first. An administrator greeted me, and as he and I walked into his office he asked me if I could pray for him. My response was, "Are you sure you want me to pray for you?" He said he did, so I asked him, "What do you want to pray about?" He told me it was personal, so I explained to him, "If you want me to pray for you I need you to be honest, because only the truth can set you free."

As I was being led by the Holy Spirit, I said, "You know, God knows all things." He replied, "I don't want people to know my business," but I assured him that I wasn't there for that. I count it as a privilege that God would choose me to pray for one of His people. The administrator then began to share with me about how he didn't like his wife. As he was explaining this, my husband arrived and I briefed him on my conversation with the administrator. The man went on to tell me that it was like he wasn't in love with his wife anymore. He told me it was a struggle for him to be with her. The Holy Spirit instructed me to ask him if he had ever had an affair. He said slowly, "Yes." I asked him how many times, and he answered me, "About three." Once again the Holy Spirit instructed me, this time telling me to have him renounce those women and the spirits that transferred into him through those sexual affairs. He agreed, so we began to pray, "Satan, I command you to be bound in Jesus' name! I renounce [he said the name of the first woman] and all the spirits that transferred from her to me in Jesus' name." Then he renounced the second woman by name. But when he got to the name of the third woman, his eyes turned red and watery and he began huffing and puffing, making sounds as he was saying the lady's name. His mouth was contorted and twisted.

Suddenly, he jumped out of the chair and landed by his desk. "I'm free! Did ya'll see that? That thing left me," he said excitedly. "It's gone! Thank you, Jesus!" There were tears in his eyes and a smile on his face.

The whole thing happened so fast that my husband and I were amazed that we didn't even have time to be afraid. The administrator thanked us, but I assured him it was the Lord who had freed him. Glory be to the one, true, living God. This is just one of many other testimonies that I could tell of how God released people from bondage that they had been under.

The Lord bought you and I with a price by laying down His life, dying on the cross, and rising from the dead on the third day. Therefore, I am grateful and will tell my testimony every day, no matter how it may sound to people or how embarrassing it might be to others. I am excited to share how God delivered me. You, too, can be free indeed from the yoke of bondage from the inside out.

Prayer for Freedom
By Michele DeCaul

THERE IS FREEDOM from demonic oppression and strongholds. The first step to being released from whatever spirits may have a stronghold in your life is to read the Word of God pray this powerful, anointed prayer, written by minister and life coach Michele DeCaul.

> *Heavenly Father, I honor You as Lord and Savior Jesus Christ! I acknowledge You as God, Creator of heaven and earth! As a sinner saved by Your love and grace, I confess that sin has entered my life through different relationships, known and unknown. I believe in my heart that Jesus Christ died on the cross and took upon Himself my sins and behaviors. I believe Jesus, who knew no sin, became sin for me so that I can live a life of freedom!*

Today I chose to honor You with gratitude and praise! Today I ask You to forgive me of all of my sins of commission, sins of omission, unknown sins, or hidden sins according to Psalm 19:12. I confess sins of doubt, fear, shame, unforgiveness, unrighteousness, distrust, idolatry, alcoholism, anger, anxiety, bad attitude, pornography, rejection, guilt, homosexuality, hopelessness, lying, manipulation, masturbation, addictions, oppression, occultism, perversion, pride, disobedience, sodomy, suicidal thoughts, abandonment, false doctrine, fornication, adultery, deception, mind disorders, and health issues. Heavenly Father, I receive Your forgiveness of my sins as You cover me with the blood of Jesus Christ.

Heavenly Father, I desire to be blessed, and I chose this day to obey Your Word and to live my life following Your Son, Jesus Christ. It is my will to be totally obedient to You and walk in truth. Give me the faith to apply everything I learn from Your Word and Holy Spirit to my life. Heavenly Father, bind Your will to my heart! Lord God, I choose this day to be a channel of blessings, not cursings. Help me to speak Your words of life instead of words of death in the name of Jesus. I submit myself to you and resist the devil, and he must flee from me! I desire to be set free from all curses over my life. I will do whatever it takes to be delivered and set free from all curses and walk in the freedom You have given me. I declare that You are the only true and living God, and there is no other God besides You. You are my source and my strength. I desire to walk in the righteousness and peace of God.

Heavenly Father, I ask You to execute divine judgment against satanic/demonic activities and help me war for my life. In the name of Jesus Christ of Nazareth, I bind all Satan's evil, wicked, demonic, lying, and tormenting spirits and strongmen. All demonic covenants, contracts, fetters, and bondages are opposed and destroyed! I declare that I am free me from all generational alliances, traditions, soul ties, and curses. I announce that all ungodly relationships, alliances, and unrighteous agreements are severed! All side effects, residual effects, influences, or curses that have been put on me, placed on me, declared over me, or decreed over me are now destroyed! All negative words, negative wishes, witchcraft prayers, ungodly soulish prayers, false prophecies, psychic prayers, spells, and every word spoken contrary to God's original plan for my life is abolished. I am free from all physiological, emotional, social, psychological, and spiritual influences that I have been exposed to or that have been passed down through generations! I declare that false memories, lies of the enemy, unrighteous instruments that have attempted to penetrate me, impressions, wrong thoughts, evil imprints, trauma, or shocks that have been revealed to me are now destroyed in the name of Jesus!

Heavenly Father, I thank You for Your unconditional love, peace, and hedge of protection around me. Your presence hides me from the enemy and any familiar spirit. I apply the blood of Jesus Christ, Psalm 91, and Your healing virtue over my relationship with You, my spirit, mind, desires, emotions, ego, my assignment, personal possessions, and everything concerning me and those divinely connected to me. In the name of Jesus I pray, amen!

Notes

1.   A police laboratory report dated June 15, 1982, states that after Butch assaulted me, "animal hairs similar to a dog" were found on both my pants and underwear. A nursing flow sheet signed on June 13, 1982, from Dickinson County Memorial Hospital reports about me, "Patient can't sleep; says when she closes her eyes she sees that horrible thing that happened to her and she doesn't want to think about it again."

I do not believe everything is a demon. We are still held accountable for our actions and decisions. No one gets away with anything.

Me and my two wonderful oldest sons after God kicked a demon out of me.
See the peace of God upon me.

To Contact the Author

Please contact the author at jcjministries@gmail.com to book her to speak at your church or event.

To share your testimony of healing after you read this book, please write to healing4thehurtingnow@live.com.